D0188218

OPENING LINES

SUSIE SHELLENBERGER · GREG JOHNSON

Nashville, Tennessee

Printed in the United States of America

4262-77
0-8054-6277-5

Dewey Decimal Classification: 306.73
Subject Heading: Dating (Social Customs)\Youth—Religious Life
Library of Congress Card Catalog Number: 95-10499

Library of Congress Cataloging-in-Publication Data

Shellenberger Susie.
Opening lines: 458 great conversation starters when you're on a date / Susie Shellenberger. Greg Johnson.
p. cm.
Summary: Provides advice about conversational techniques that teenagers can use in their dating as they seek to keep their vows of abstinence and maintain their spiritual values.
ISBN 0-8054-6277-5 (pb)
1. Dating (Social customs)—Miscellanea—Juvenile literature. 2. Conversation—Miscellanea—Juvenile literature. 3. Youth—Conduct of life—Miscellanea—Juvenile literature. 4. Christian life—Miscellanea—Juvenile literature. [1. Dating (Social customs) 2. Christian life.] I. Johnson, Greg, 1956- . II. Title
HQ801.S5243 1995
306.73—dc20
95-10499
CIP
AC

To Scott, Brett, and Matt Shellenberger, my three favorite guys
who never run out of fun things to talk about!
Love,
Susie

WHAT CAN WE TALK ABOUT?

Have you taken the "True Love Waits" challenge yet?

Are you going to be one of the millions of teens throughout North America who has the courage to say, "I'm choosing to wait until the honeymoon"?

Do you want to know how to be a total success with the opposite sex?

Did you read our other book, *258 Great Dates While You Wait?*

Are you getting sick of all these questions and wish the book would get started?

Hey, if you're sick of questions, this isn't the book for you. That's all that's in this book!

Why would anyone write a book filled with questions?

Good question!

We believe that if guys and girls are going to date—either in groups or one-on-one—and

they're committed to sexual purity, then it's a good idea to have something to talk about when they're together.

Yeah, we know. TALKING to the opposite sex can sometimes be kind of scary. But once you get the *other* person TALKING, a real conversation actually takes place. And that's FUN! But how do you start a conversation? By asking questions. We're not talking about yes or no questions that allow fast, no-brain responses. We challenge you to ask *thinking* questions—stuff that demands some thought. It's *these* kinds of questions that will turn small talk into

interesting conversations—and perhaps even a close friendship.

Here's the truth (and if you don't believe us, ask ANYONE): Unless you have good conversation skills, any relationship you have will soon degenerate. You'll either spend all of your time looking at a colored rectangle (the TV or a movie), or you'll be stuck on a couch or in a car with nothing to do besides communicate through touch. Both spell t-r-o-u-b-l-e.

So let's get a fun conversation going! Where do you start? With questions. And that's where we come in.

This book contains a fairly extensive list of questions. Here's a few tips on how to use it:

1. Read through the questions before each date and pick out ten to twenty to talk about.

2. Photocopy or write down a list of questions to take with you when you're out with someone.

3. Take the book! Hey, it's kinda cool lookin', and it'll show the one you're with

that you take people and relationships seriously. Besides the questions, you might want to take along a copy of *258 Great Dates.* It's filled with tons of incredibly creative dating ideas. You're sure to find something that fits what you like to do. You could wind up planning out the next three months worth of weekends! (And divide up who's going to pay for which one.)

4. Use these questions to spark other questions you might think of, and then you're off and running on great conversations, both fun and serious!

One thing you should know: Many of these questions have an agenda. That is, they are the type of questions that will tell you something you absolutely have to know about the person you're spending time with. Of course, some of the questions are just fun. But others will give you insight on your friend's values, true character, and how he or she will respond in certain situations.

So here's your assignment: Grab a pen or pencil. (That's right, go get one . . . now! We'll wait.)

(Thank you.)

As you read through these questions, circle

the ones you want to make part of your "conversation repertoire." (That's French for "questions you want to have stored in your brain for future use.") That way you won't have to read this book a dozen times looking for great questions—not that you *shouldn't* read this book a dozen times. It's just that you probably have a more important book to read a dozen times or more—like the Bible!

Read it through, and then use it to ask lots of questions. And have a great time getting to know the opposite sex.

P.S. These questions are in no particular

order, but you'll find a symbol beside each one that puts it into a category. Use the symbols to find certain types of questions, or just find your favorite questions, regardless of the subject. Here are the symbols:

 Choices

 Situations

 Family

 Dating

 Money

 Spirituality

 Friends

 Love

 Future

 Personality

 Just for fun

If you had to give up one of your five senses (sight, hearing, taste, touch, smell), which would you choose to live without?

If you had to have either two noses, three eyes, or four feet, which would you choose to add to your body?

What have you learned about God lately? How did you learn it?

Do you think it's okay to "pull the plug" on someone who's terminally ill and wants to die?

What do you think makes a good date?
A bad date?

If you suddenly won a million dollars, how would you spend it?

If you could receive truthful answers to any two questions, *what* would you ask and to *whom* would you ask it?

What do you enjoy most about your life?
What would you like to change?

How do you handle compliments?

Do you believe a person has to be baptized with water to really be a Christian?

How would you react if a stranger approached you and offered to carry your groceries to your car?

Is it always wrong to kill?
What about insects?
Animals?

If you had to live in one of these places, which one would you choose: Antarctica or Siberia?

If you could be a contestant on any TV game show, which would you choose?

Which of these old TV *titles* (not shows, but titles) best describes your life right now?
(1) "Growing Pains"
(2) "The Wonder Years"
(3) "Who's the Boss?"
(4) "Little Rascals"

What's something you could do for one of your teachers tomorrow that would really make his or her day?

Would you be willing to have super-frightening dreams every night for three years if it meant you'd be really popular the rest of your life?

Do you think there's life on other planets?

If *you* were Eve, would *you* have eaten the forbidden fruit?

If *you* were Adam, would *you* have blamed it on *Eve?*

If you would receive $5,000 for doing one of the following for an entire week, which would you choose?

(1) dig ditches
(2) wash dishes in a leper hospital
(3) clean gorilla cages.

- Do you believe each person has a guardian angel?

- Is Sunday School important? Why or why not?

- Do you think we will go straight to heaven or hell when we die, or will we stay in the ground until Christ returns?

If you could invent a brand-new chewing gum, what would you call it?

How would it differ from all other gum on the market?

What flavor would it be?

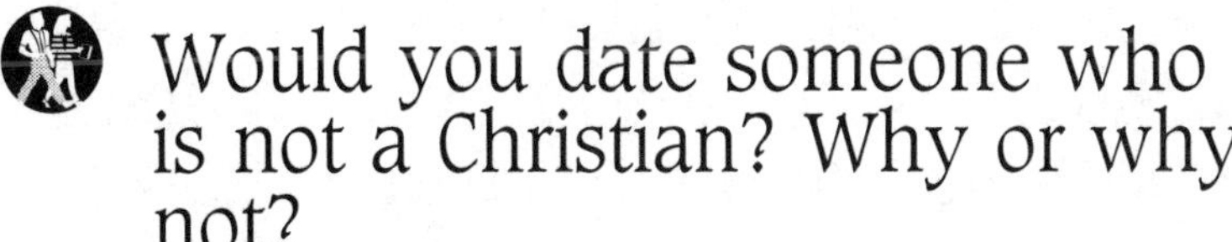

Would you date someone who is not a Christian? Why or why not?

Would you rather command a ship, plane, or tank in war?

What's the most frightening thing that has ever happened to you so far?

Do you think anyone ever cleans out water towers? If you were offered a job working on top of and inside a water tower, what fears, questions, or doubts would you have?

If you could host your own TV talk show, what would you call it? Who are the first ten guests you'd like to interview?

If you could ask contemporary Christian artist Amy Grant any two questions, what would you ask her?

What's one thing your parents were right about after all?

Have you ever memorized any Bible verses?

Can you share a memorized one with me right now?

If you could be supplied with one of these items free for a whole year, which would you choose?

(1) athletic shoes

(2) sweaters

(3) sweatshirts

(4) hats

What makes you laugh uncontrollably?

What would you be more frightened of, a snake, a lion, or a tarantula?

Do you have a friend who's always late?

How does that make you feel?

Have you ever talked with him or her about it?

What's something (like the above) that *you* always do, and you're wondering if a friend is ever going to talk with *you* about?

What's your favorite church hymn?
Favorite chorus?
Favorite camp song?

If you had to choose between TV and radio, which would you do without for an entire year?

What's your favorite color?

If you could assign a color to happiness, what color would it be?
What about fear?

What's the difference between encouraging someone and complimenting someone?

If you could write a book, what would you title it? What would it be about?
How much would you sell it for?

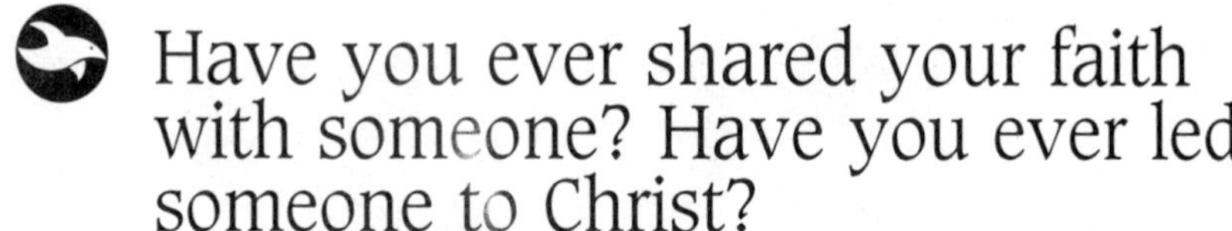

Have you ever shared your faith with someone? Have you ever led someone to Christ?

Do you feel uncomfortable inviting people to church? Do you think it's important to do so?

What's the most recent book you've read?

If you won an all-expenses paid trip to anywhere in the world, where would you go and why?

What's the most exciting thing going on in your life *right now*?

If you would receive $100 to do one of the following, which would you choose?

(1) skydiving
(2) hang-gliding
(3) wind-surfing
(4) para-sailing

Do you believe in demons?

Have you ever been to another country?
Which one?
What differences did you notice?
Would you like to go back?

When was the last time you cried?
Why?

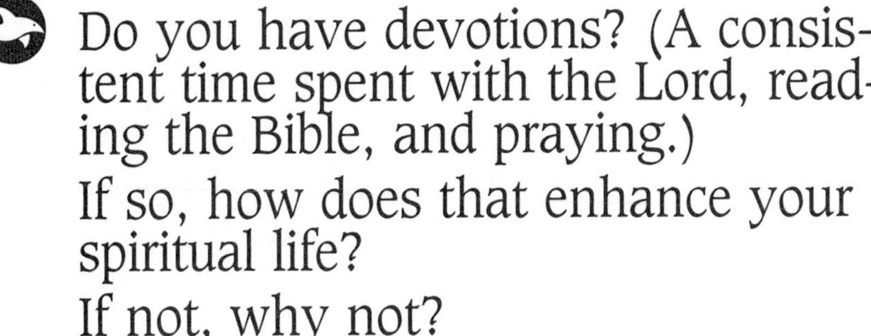

Do you have devotions? (A consistent time spent with the Lord, reading the Bible, and praying.)

If so, how does that enhance your spiritual life?

If not, why not?

Do you think it was easier or more difficult for people during Bible times to follow God than it is now?

If someone in your family needed one of your kidneys, how would you feel about donating it to him or her?

If you could take a doctor-prescribed pill that would put you to sleep for a solid week, then give you incredible energy for a whole month, would you do it knowing you'd miss out on everything for one week?

What version of the Bible do you read?

Would you rather drive an ice-cream truck or deliver singing telegrams?

Have you ever broken a bone? If so, how?

What was your favorite children's book?

Do you think it's ethical to help someone die who's in constant pain and doesn't want to live any longer?

If you could be a cartoon, who would you become?

Have you ever thought of designing your own athletic shoes?
What would the soles look like?
Squiggly lines?
Round spots?
Raised cleats?

When was the last time you read something from the Bible?

Have you ever had surgery?

What's your biggest pet peeve?

What do you not understand about the Bible that you'd like to ask someone about?

Have you asked anyone?

Why not?

Who do you think would have the answer to this question?

Will you try to get your question answered *this week?*

Do you think you've ever had contact with an angel?

Are you an exaggerator?

If so, why?

What things do you tend to exaggerate the most?

Would you ever serenade someone outside his or her bedroom window?

What would you sing?

Would you be embarrassed?

How would you feel if they didn't like it?

What specific thing can you do for a friend to reflect Jesus to him or her?

If your best friend hired a sky-writer to place a message in the sky about you, what would it say? What would your first-period teacher say in such a message? Your parents?

What could you learn from an eighty-five-year-old man?

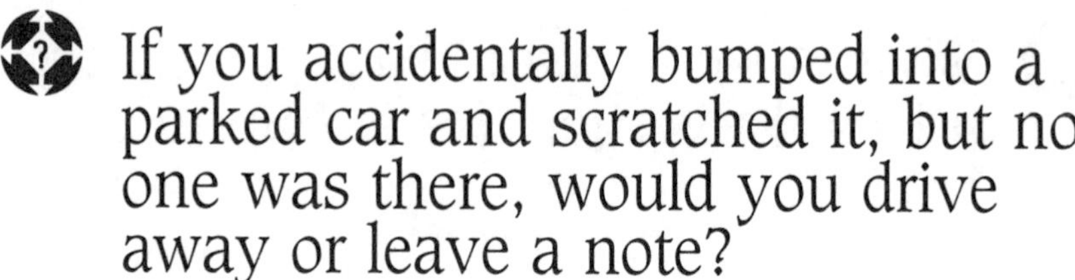

If you accidentally bumped into a parked car and scratched it, but no one was there, would you drive away or leave a note?

Have you ever attended a funeral? How did you feel?

What's the best prank you've ever played on someone? What's the best prank that has ever been played on *you?*

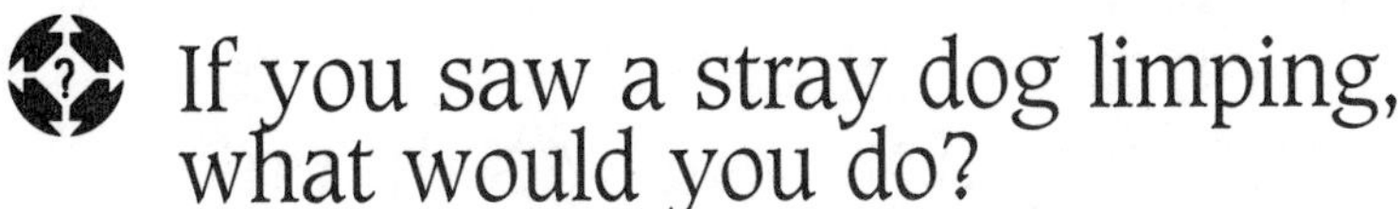

If you saw a stray dog limping, what would you do?

Do you believe Christians can live holy lives?

Do you get your energy from being with other people or from being alone?

What's the best vacation you've ever taken?

If you had unlimited resources, what would you like to invent?

Do you want your spouse to be smarter and more attractive than you, or less intelligent and less attractive?

What's your favorite holiday?

Why?

Does your family have any annual traditions associated with this holiday?

Would you be willing to be completely alone—as in totally isolated—for an entire year if you would receive $25,000 when the year was up?

Do you believe it's important for Christians to take communion (or Lord's Supper)?
What does taking communion mean to you?

Would you give up your citizenship and be willing to never return to your country if it meant you'd be world-famous and would live in luxury?

What's the difference between God, Jesus Christ, and the Holy Spirit?

What are two goals you have for your life?
How do you plan to reach them?

What's the best dream you've ever had while sleeping?

Do you dream in color or black and white?

Do you usually remember your dreams?

When a waitress or waiter is rude to you, how does it make you feel?

Are you tempted to return rudeness with rudeness?

How *should* you respond?

Would you rather be over- or under-dressed at your best friend's birthday party?

At the symphony?

At an expensive restaurant?

At McDonald's?

At church?

At a funeral?

At a wedding?

What's your favorite place to eat and why?

When did you last eat there?

Do you believe being involved in church is important?

What do you love most about *your* church?

Is attendance important?

If, after purchasing several items in a department store, you notice that you were not charged for an item that was under $1, would you return and report the oversight?

What if it were a $20 item?

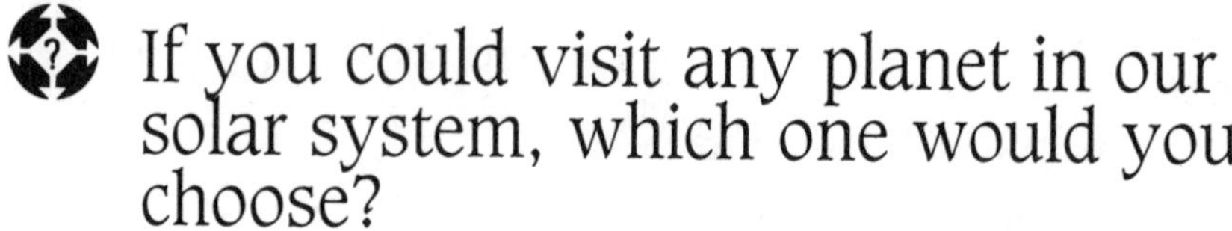

If you could visit any planet in our solar system, which one would you choose?

Are you afraid of God's judgment?

Would you be willing to clean toilets for two solid years without pay if it would mean world peace?

What's one thing you wish your parents understood better about you? Your teachers?

What was your favorite outdoor children's game?

What's your favorite Scripture?

Would you rather have a cheeseburger, fries, and a Coke, or turkey and dressing, veggies, and iced-tea?

Do you expect more or less of others than you do of yourself?

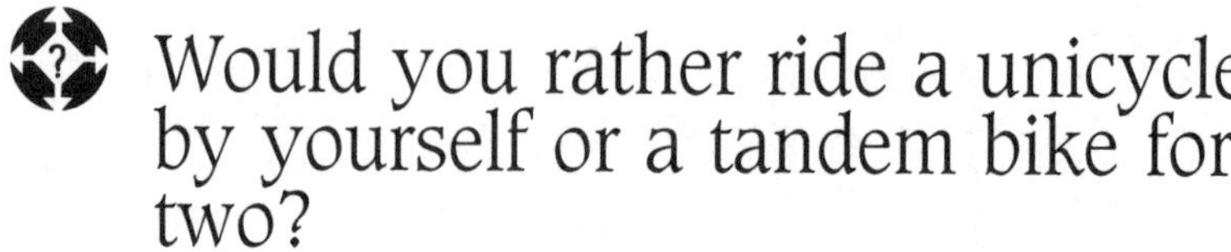
Would you rather ride a unicycle by yourself or a tandem bike for two?

Do you ever sing to yourself? When was the last time?

Would you rather
(1) perform in a play
(2) perform in a band concert
(3) perform magic tricks
(4) perform on a TV cooking show?

What helps you grow closer to Christ?
What things interfere with your spiritual life?

If your fiancee became paralyzed a month before your wedding, would you go through with it or cancel?

What's your favorite outdoor sport?
Indoor sport?
Group sport?
Individual sport?

What one question will you be sure to ask God when you meet Him?

Is there anyone you'd want to trade lives with? Who? Why or why not?

Are your closest friends guys or girls?

What makes it hardest for you to be all God wants you to be?

Describe an instance when someone really let you down?

How did you feel?

Did you hold a grudge or forgive and forget?

Would you be willing to donate parts of your body to science after you die?

How would you feel if your parents wanted *their* bodies donated to science?

If you were president, what ten things would you try to do to make things better (and how would you do them)?

When it comes to punishment from parents (or school), who has it tougher, guys or girls?

How good are your parents at keeping their promises?

Do you like your friends to be brutally honest with you?

What positive things would they say about you?

Any specific areas in your life that need a little more attention?

What do you like best: teachers who are fun, but don't teach very well, or teachers who are strict, but are good instructors?

Are you ever embarrassed to be around your parents?

What things do they do that bug you?

Do you ever think other kids' parents do dumb stuff, or do you not care or notice?

When you make mistakes, is it easy for you to accept blame, or do you find yourself blaming others?

If you could go back in time, what period of history would you choose?

Why?

How good are you at keeping secrets?

Do you think there is anyone who looks up to you?

How do you feel about being someone's role model?

What are the top-five best times you've had with your mom and dad?

With your siblings or other relatives?

What bugs you most about kids at school?

What food would you rather not ever see again your entire life?

What food could you eat every day of your entire life?

Can you remember a time when you got into trouble by telling a lie?

What was the punishment?

Did you deserve it?

Do you like to listen to gossip and keep it to yourself, or pass along what you've heard, or ignore it altogether?

What's your curfew?

How did you and your folks come up with it?

Have you ever missed it?

What happened?

When you're mad at someone, what *little,* annoying things do you do to get back at them?

Or are you the type who gets back in a *big* way?

 What would you rather have from your mom or dad: more gifts or more time?

 What is the worst dream you've ever had?

Do you snore, talk, grind your teeth, move around a lot, or sleep too hard to know?

 Have you ever thought how you'd act if you found out you were adopted?

Do you think it should make any difference?

If you lived to be very old, would you rather lose some of your memory or all of your physical capabilities?

If you agreed with one person on a price for your car (or other prized possession), then someone else offered you more, what would you do?

If you were at work and saw a fellow employee steal some money, what would you do?

If there is one talent you wished you had, what would it be?

Do you ever find yourself getting jealous of others because of the talents *they* have?

Do you pay attention to the way other people dress, or do you even notice?

If you talked about things in your life that you fail at, do you think your friends would like you less or more?

What type of people do you like to be around most: those who act like they have it all together, or those who are honest about their shortcomings?

Would you date someone more than two years younger or older than you?

Do you ever wish you were an adult right now?
What do you look forward to most in your adult life?

What are the best things about being a teenager?

Have you ever had a nickname?
If you had one now, what would you like it to be?

What would you recommend to the principal to try to make the school better? (Seriously.)

What are some things you've heard from people about God that you know or think aren't true?

If you could change anything about your parents, what would it be?

Out of everything you do, what makes you feel the proudest?

What qualities make up a best friend?

Is there anything a best friend can do to ruin a friendship?

Would you rather your parents were poor and spent time with you, or rich and working all the time?

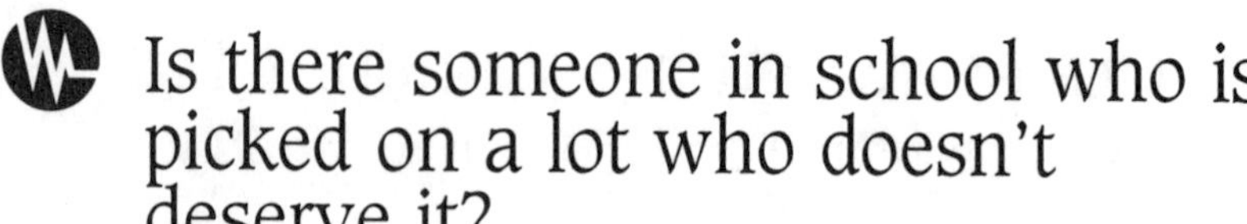

Is there someone in school who is picked on a lot who doesn't deserve it?

Have you ever tried to do anything to stop it?

What *could* you do?

What bores you the most?

Is there anyone you trust so much you could tell them your deepest, most private thoughts?

Would you rather be surprised or know what you're getting for presents?

How do you feel when you see people from other countries less fortunate than you on TV?

Have you or your family ever tried to do anything to help them?

Are we responsible to help others along the way?

Do you ever think about death? What do you think heaven and hell will be like?

When was the last time you were so angry you could hardly control yourself?

How do you normally handle your anger?

What classes at school do you think will be completely useless to you in the future?

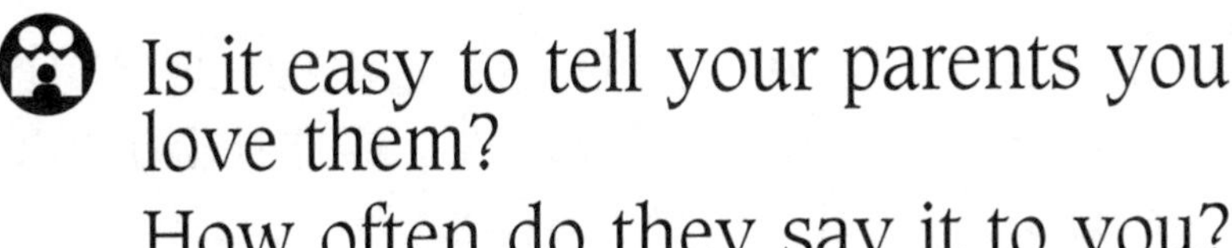

Is it easy to tell your parents you love them?
How often do they say it to you?

What's the toughest part about being a teenager?

What's the luckiest thing that has ever happened to you?
Do you believe in luck?

If the parents of one of your friends were getting a divorce, what advice would you give him to help him get through it?

What would you do if you caught your best friend telling a lie?

What things do you think are worth standing up for?

What consequences are you willing to face for standing up for your beliefs?

When you have a question that's really personal, who do you discuss it with?

What do you think of people who act like chameleons (You know, they blend into their surroundings by being a different person at school, home, and church)?

If you had a friend who told you she was pregnant, how would you react, and what advice would you give her?

What were your hobbies or collections while you were growing up?

What's the most valuable thing you own?

What do you think about guys who have to fight to prove something?

Would you rather be famous and rich, or someone who helps a lot of people?
Why?

What do your parents believe about alcohol? Gambling?

What do you think people would say about you at your ten-year high school reunion if you weren't around?

What would you *want* them to say?

What things in life have eternal value?

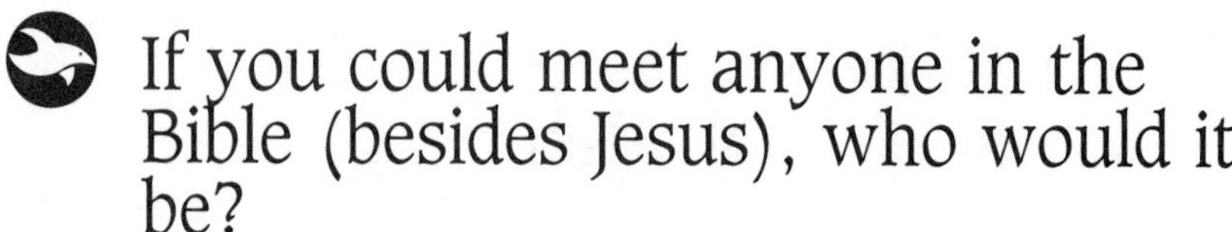

If you could meet anyone in the Bible (besides Jesus), who would it be?

When you do something stupid or embarrassing, how do you react? Do you act like it's no big deal, or do you do something to put the attention on someone else?

Have you thought about what you'd do if our country had to go to war and the government began drafting men and women again?

In what type of war would you fight?

Have you made a commitment to yourself and to God to remain sexually abstinent until marriage?

Why or why not?

If so, do you think it is important to tell your family and friends?

Why or why not?

- What's your favorite thing to do on Saturday mornings?

- What are a few of your all-time favorite movies?
  TV shows?
  Songs?
  Music groups?

- Who are your heroes—people you've looked up to over the years?

◐ If you could change anything about the way you look or act, what would it be?

◐ When you don't understand something in school, do you ask questions or remain quiet?

◐ Are you a morning or evening person?

◐ Are you a country or a city person at heart?

How important is being popular to you?

To what length have you noticed friends at school going to be popular?

Why do they do that?

What does it mean to you to have a good self-image?

What do you think of yourself . . . *really*?

◐ What things do you do that give you the best feeling inside?

Have you ever picked on or talked about someone so much that you felt bad about it later?

Do you and your parents ever sit down and talk about things other than the daily stuff?

If something makes you sad, are you able to cry?

If something is really funny, are you able to laugh out loud?

What characteristics do you want in someone you date?

In a marriage partner?

Do you think your parents still make time for you?

Are you friendly enough with them that they think you want to spend time with them?

Have your parents ever asked you to quit spending time with a certain friend?

Were they fair?

How did you react?

If you knew (or know) anyone with AIDS, how would (or do) you react?

What do you think you could do for him or her?

Do you think your parents would rather you get better grades by cheating or lesser grades by not cheating?

Have you ever given away any of your own money?

How did it make you feel?

If you knew you could save the lives of twenty people in another country, would you go without new clothes and spending money for an entire year?

If a good friend was getting into trouble and you were the only one who knew, what would you do?

What would you be willing to practice if you knew you could one day be the best in the school at it? Do you have that kind of dedication in anything?

Do you think it is fair to bring a child into the world before you are married? Why or why not?

Have either of your parents ever lost his or her job?

What would you do to help the family if either of them did?

What would you say to a friend who told you she (or he) had been physically abused by someone else?

What motivates you the most in school: pleasing your parents, pleasing your teachers, a tangible reward at the end, or the inner satisfaction of doing it yourself?

 Have you ever been so bummed-out on life that you wanted to run away?

What did you do or how did you get out of that mood?

◐ Are you so ultra-competitive that you have to win . . . or can you enjoy a game just for the fun of it?

◐ What things used to embarrass you a lot?

How about now?

Would you rather work on a team to achieve a goal (a completed report, a team sport), or would you rather do it alone and get the credit for yourself?

What things in school come easy for you and which ones are tougher?

What are you going through now that your parents say they understand because they went through it when they were your age?

Do you think they really understand you?

If you were given $10,000 to help other people, where would you spend it?

What disappoints your parents most about you?
How do you feel about that?

What is most important to you: looks, talent, or brains?

What is the difference between love and lust?

What have you been taught about the differences between races (if anything)?

How can people turn their "weaknesses" into strengths that can help them or others?

What makes you more uncomfortable when you watch TV or movies: sex, violence, or bad language?

If you could have an experience that you'd remember the rest of your life, or a cool possession you'd use for a short time, which would you rather have?

Do you think sex outside of marriage is wrong?
Why or why not?

What do you think it takes to make and keep friends?
Are you the type of person who can do that?

What's the craziest thing you've ever done?

Would you do it again?

If you could know the future—but not have the power to change it—would you want to know it?

After college, do you hope you'll have a job that is fun and fulfilling or a job that pays a lot?

Have you ever thought about going into full-time ministry?

What gifts do you think God has given you to serve Him?

If you had some friends who were mad at each other, what would you do to try to make things right?

How do you express true love to God?

To yourself?

To your friends?

To your parents?

To your future mate (even though you may not know who they will be)?

How would you feel if you were in an accident that caused you to lose the use of your legs?

How would you react?

Would you blame God?

Have you ever gone on a "media fast" where you didn't watch TV, listen to music, or go to movies? How would you fill your time if you did this? (Why don't you try it?)

What does real love mean to you?

What animal describes you best?

Do you think the world will be better or worse by the time you're raising kids?

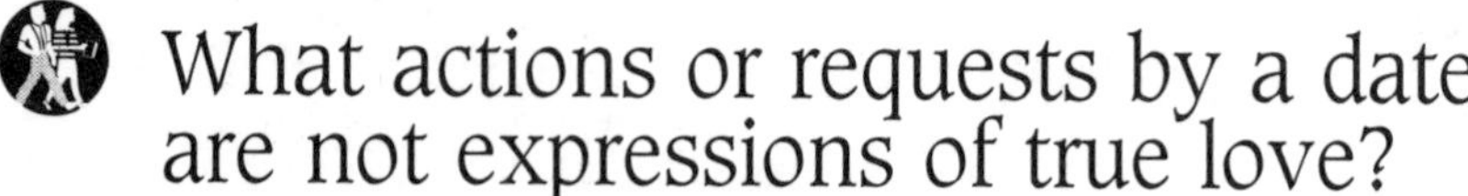

What actions or requests by a date are not expressions of true love?

Why do you think some girls date older guys?

How does that make guys feel?

In what ways are girls more mature than guys?

Guys than girls?

Is there someone at school you'd like to befriend but so far haven't been able to?

Do they know about it?

Have you ever been friends with someone who was teased or picked on a lot?

How did that affect the way you treated them?

What experiences have you had that make you believe in a kind and loving God?

Is there anything in the world that makes you doubt this?

What things should parents do without expecting you to thank them?

What gift of love would you like to give your future children?

How often and in what ways do you express appreciation to your folks for what they do?

What types of things should be so important that your parents bug you about them?

What do you think makes a good teacher?

A bad teacher?

When you see someone in a wheelchair or someone who walks or talks differently, how does it make you feel?

Have you ever had a real conversation with someone about their "handicap"?

If a good friend had done something really bad and hadn't gotten caught, what would you do (knowing that he'll probably keep doing it until he gets caught)?

What would be the positives and negatives of being best friends with someone blind or disabled?

Do you say what people want to hear or what you really think?

How do you show a person love without having sex?

Sometimes friends act like each other. Do you try to act like *them* more than they act like *you?*

Have you ever had a teacher or another adult make you feel like a fool?

What did you do after they did?

What were your fears when you were a kid?

How about now?

If you could address the whole school for fifteen minutes, what would you want to say and why?

What are the best things about having brothers and sisters?

The worst?

How do you feel when you hear your parents argue?
Do you listen or go off somewhere so you can't hear?

Do you have a clean room or an "organizationally impaired" one? What do your parents have to say about it?

Is there anything that scares you even though you know there is no reason you should be frightened?

Are you the type who will try anything once?

If you try and "fail" at something, are you less likely to try it again, or does it make you want to succeed at it all the more?

How do you feel about movie and record ratings for teenagers? For pre-teens?

If you were a coach and the people who played for you didn't listen to what you were saying, what would you do and how would you do it?

◐ What does being contented mean to you?
Do you ever feel that way?
When?

◐ What's the difference between happiness and joy?

What are the five most important things to know if you're baby-sitting an infant?

A toddler?

A grade schooler?

Do you like your name? What would you change it to if you could?

Have you always felt that way?

Parents are supposed to set "guardrails" to protect their children so they don't "go over the edge." What are the top five rules your parents won't budge on? Do you think this is fair?

How do you act when you get a gift you don't really like?

Have you ever given someone a "recycled" gift—something someone else had given you that you didn't like?

What does the word "discernment" mean to you?

Have you ever been excluded by friends from something you really wanted to go to?
How did you feel?
What did you do?

Would you rather be an average basketball player on a great basketball team or an all-star tennis player?

Why do some people not believe in God?

If you were to die, what would your family miss most about you?

Who can you be brutally honest with?
Why?

What kind of pet do you have? What's your favorite thing about it?

If you don't have a pet, what kind would you like to have?

What really gets on your nerves?

What's the best possible thing that could happen to you today?

How about the worst?

Do you ever see your mom or dad express deep emotion?
How does it make you feel?

Who is it easy to cry in front of?
Not so easy?

What do you dislike most about yourself?
Do you believe other people know (or care) about it?

Have you ever done anything particularly brave?

When you're daydreaming, what things do you imagine yourself doing that others would notice?

What do you think is the best part about being a parent?
The worst?

If you could give your parents one piece of advice, what would it be?

Have you ever asked your parents who you would live with if both of them died?

Should you have a say in that?

If one of your friends had a close relative who died, what would you do?

Have you ever lied to keep a good friend from getting into trouble at school?

With the law?

With their parents?

Would you want someone to lie for you if you were about to get into trouble?

For what things will you try to play one parent against the other so you can get your way?

 Do you ever think about going to war?

Would you go if you were drafted?

 What gifts could you give your parents that they would treasure for their entire lives?

 Have you ever been tempted to smoke cigarettes?

What did you do?

How about drinking or taking drugs?

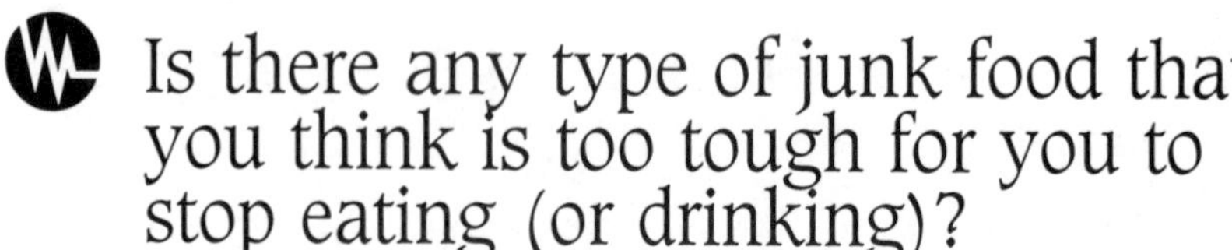

Is there any type of junk food that you think is too tough for you to stop eating (or drinking)?

What are some of the most important things about life that you've learned this past year?

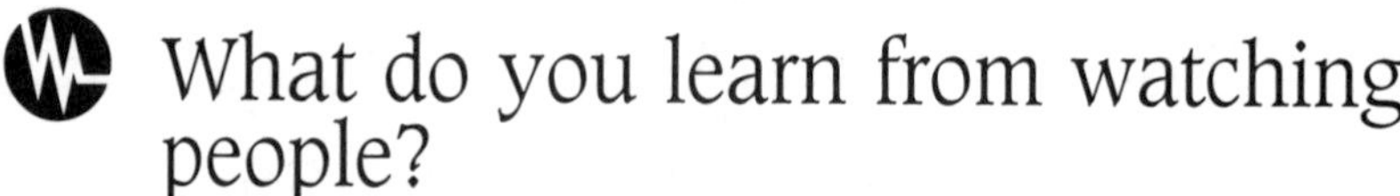

What do you learn from watching people?

If you could eat something that would never make you depressed, sad, or lonely again, would you eat it?

Join hundreds of thousands of young people that have made a commitment to sexual abstinence. As an expression of your commitment, make a copy of this card and keep it as a reminder of your decision.

We would like to know of your decision as well as support and encourage you in the days ahead. Please give your name and address and mail this card to True Love Waits (MSN 152), 127 Ninth Avenue North, Nashville, TN 37234. If you have questions, call 1-800-LUV-WAIT.

TRUE LOVE WAITS

Believing that true love waits, I make a commitment to God, myself, my family, my friends, my future mate, and my future children to be sexually abstinent from this day until the day I enter a biblical marriage relationship.

Signed:______________________________

Dated:______________________________

Name:____________________________________

Address:__________________________________

City:________________ State:____ Zip:________

PLACE
STAMP HERE
The Post Office
will not deliver
mail without
postage

True Love Waits (MSN 152)
127 Ninth Avenue North
Nashville, TN 37234